This book belongs to

_ _ _ _ _ _ _ _ _ _ _ _ _ _

_ _ _ _ _ _ _ _ _ _ _ _ _ _

_ _ _ _ _ _ _ _ _ _ _ _ _ _

_ _ _ _ _ _ _ _ _ _ _ _ _ _

Published in 2020 by
agnes & aubrey
1st Floor, Unit D,
Emperor House, Dragonfly Place
London SE4 2FL

www.agnesandaubrey.com
hello@agnesandaubrey.com

First published in the UK in 2019 as "Take Me On Holiday:
The Young Explorer's Guide to Every Holiday in the World"

A CIP catalogue record of this book is available
from the British Library

ISBN 978-1-9164745-6-7 (North American edition)

This edition distributed by
Consortium Book Sales & Distribution, Inc.,
part of the Ingram Content Group

Thanks to:
David, Arlo, Zubin, Quincy, and Viola Schweitzer;
Monika Loewy; Oliver Grieb, and Megan Cabot

Printed in China on paper
from responsible sources

MIX
Paper from
responsible sources
FSC® C124385

# take me on vacation

The YOUNG EXPLORER's guide
to EVERY VACATION in the world

by mary richards

agnes & aubrey

# ALL ABOUT THIS BOOK

You can use this book wherever you are going!
It will help you:

>> PREPARE for your trip.

>> EXPLORE your new surroundings.

>> REMEMBER all the fun you've had!

The book is divided into five color-coded ADVENTURE CHAPTERS. Every time you go on vacation, start a new ADVENTURE. Throughout the book you will also find FACTS about vacations, traveling, and places all around the world.

The paper in the book has a rough texture which is perfect for writing and drawing with a PENCIL.
(A marker pen might be a bit too inky.)

You can start your adventure RIGHT HERE! >>>>>>>

draw your face here

Your NAME

- - - - - - - - - - - - - - - - - - - - - - - - - - - - - - - - -

Your ADDRESS

- - - - - - - - - - - - - - - - - - - - - - - - - - - - - - - - -

The DATE you started this book

- - - - - - - - - - - - - - - - - - - - - - - - - - - - - - - - -

Your favorite PLACES TO VISIT

- - - - - - - - - - - - - - - - - - - - - - - - - - - - - - - - -

- - - - - - - - - - - - - - - - - - - - - - - - - - - - - - - - -

- - - - - - - - - - - - - - - - - - - - - - - - - - - - - - - - -

The places you'd MOST LIKE TO DISCOVER

- - - - - - - - - - - - - - - - - - - - - - - - - - - - - - - - -

# THINKING ABOUT VACATIONS

A vacation is a time when we are free from our normal daily routine - and we don't have to go to school or work. In some parts of the world, they use the word "holiday" instead.

Vacations can be enjoyed at home, exploring the local area. They are a great opportunity for looking at our surroundings with fresh eyes and appreciating the cities and countryside all around us.

On vacation, we can also travel and visit new places. We might stay with people we know already, or go to a hotel, rental home, or summer camp - and make new friends.

Over the past 150 years the invention of trains, ocean liners, ferries, and airplanes have opened up the number of places we are able to travel to.

In recent times, the internet has made booking vacations online easier for everyone across the world. As a result, we are able to travel more - and further - than people in the past. The internet also allows us to search out pictures of famous destinations and see the world from the comfort of our own homes!

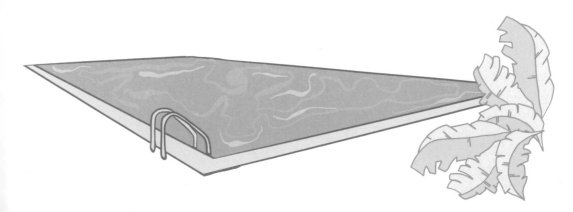

# ALL ABOUT JOURNEYS

Some destinations are very easy to reach, but others are much more difficult!

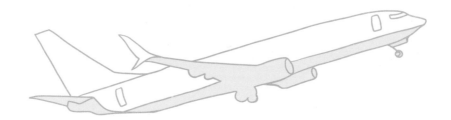

AIRPLANES are the quickest way to travel from one side of the world to the other. Flights to faraway places are called "long haul."

The first STEAM TRAINS appeared in the 19th century, and changed the way people traveled. It was now possible to journey to places far from the hustle and bustle of city life.

OCEAN LINERS were also invented in the 19th century and powered by steam. They could transport passengers between continents.

RMS Queen Mary sailed across the Atlantic from 1936 to 1967. At the time it was the largest ship ever built - turned on its end, it was taller than the Empire State Building in New York. It's now a floating museum.

These days, huge CRUISE SHIPS operate all over the world, stopping off in many different places on one trip.

Many people choose to go on vacation by CAR.

A journey in a car is very straightforward, as you can take all your belongings with you. You don't have to rely on timetables - you can travel at any time. CARS and BUSES load onto FERRIES if they need to travel across seas as well as on land.

# VACATION ACTIVITIES

A vacation is a good time for trying new things!
Here are some things you might do on vacation
- whether you're traveling far from home or
staying in your local area.

### ENJOY LOCAL FESTIVALS

In Brazil, Carnival is celebrated
every year in the week before the
beginning of Lent (usually in
late February). The party lasts
for six days, as people dress up
in colorful costumes and parade
through the streets.

### VISIT A MUSEUM

Millions of people visit
museums every year. The Tate
gallery in St Ives, on the
South-West tip of England is
perfect for a vacation visit,
as it's located right on the
beach!

## LOOK AT WILDLIFE

Madagascar is famous for being home to 100 species of lemur. They don't live anywhere else in the world - but when you're on vacation you might spot one in a ZOO.

## PLAY A NEW SPORT

A vacation is a good time to get active and try something different!

## SAMPLE LOCAL FOOD

Sushi is popular all over the world but it originated in Japan. It's made from fine cuts of raw fish laid on rice and often wrapped in rolls of seaweed.

What VACATION ACTIVITY would you most like to do?

- - - - - - - - - - - - - - - - - - - - - - - - - - - - - - - - - - - - -

Save this space to draw a special vacation moment! What is it?

# ADVENTURE NO.1

VACATION DESTINATION:

- - - - - - - - - - - - - - - - - - - - - - - - - - - - - -

DATES you'll be away:

- - - - - - - - - - - - - - - - - - - - - - - - - - - - - -

WHO are you traveling with? Are you VISITING anyone?

- - - - - - - - - - - - - - - - - - - - - - - - - - - - - -

- - - - - - - - - - - - - - - - - - - - - - - - - - - - - -

What are you HOPING TO SEE?

- - - - - - - - - - - - - - - - - - - - - - - - - - - - - -

- - - - - - - - - - - - - - - - - - - - - - - - - - - - - -

How are you GETTING THERE?

- - - - - - - - - - - - - - - - - - - - - - - - - - - - - -

# PLANNING YOUR TRIP

Find out a little about the place you're going to.

What's the WEATHER usually like at this time?

- - - - - - - - - - - - - - - - - - - - - - - - - - - - - - - - -

- - - - - - - - - - - - - - - - - - - - - - - - - - - - - - - - -

Is it famous for any particular FOOD or DRINK?

- - - - - - - - - - - - - - - - - - - - - - - - - - - - - - - - -

- - - - - - - - - - - - - - - - - - - - - - - - - - - - - - - - -

What ANIMALS live there?

- - - - - - - - - - - - - - - - - - - - - - - - - - - - - - - - -

- - - - - - - - - - - - - - - - - - - - - - - - - - - - - - - - -

Do any FAMOUS PEOPLE come from this place?

- - - - - - - - - - - - - - - - - - - - - - - - - - - - - - - - -

DRAW a MAP of the place you're visiting HERE.

You could mark on it:

>> Important towns or cities.
>> Any rivers, lakes, or seas.
>> The place you'll be staying.

# PACKING LIST

Let's work out what you'll need for your trip.
How long will you be staying?

-------------------------------------------------------------

DRAW your BAG or SUITCASE here!

CIRCLE all the things you'll need to take with you!

socks (how many?)_ _ _ _ _ _       tops (how many?) _ _ _ _ _ _

underwear (how many?) _ _ _       pants (how many?)    _ _ _ _

pajamas (how many?) _ _ _ _       skirts (how many?) _ _ _ _ _

| | | |
|---|---|---|
| warm coat | raincoat | sweater |
| beanie | gloves | scarf |
| toothbrush | toothpaste | soap |
| bathing suit | goggles | bodyboard |
| sunglasses | sunscreen | sunhat |
| shoes | sandals | boots |

>> Make a note of anything else you'll need:

- - - - - - - - - - - - - - - - - - - - - - - - - - - - -

- - - - - - - - - - - - - - - - - - - - - - - - - - - - -

- - - - - - - - - - - - - - - - - - - - - - - - - - - - -

- - - - - - - - - - - - - - - - - - - - - - - - - - - - -

You'll also want to pack THIS BOOK!

# GETTING THERE

How are you getting to your DESTINATION?

Circle as many ways of traveling as you need to:

>> CAR          >> CAMPERVAN or R.V.

>> BUS          >> AIRPLANE

>> BOAT         >> TRAIN

How FAR will you be traveling?

- - - - - - - - - - - - - miles

How LONG will your journey take?

- - - - - - - - - - - - - - -

Will you be passing through any places on the way?
Make a list of them:

- - - - - - - - - - - - - - - - - - - - - - - - - - - - - - -

- - - - - - - - - - - - - - - - - - - - - - - - - - - - - - -

- - - - - - - - - - - - - - - - - - - - - - - - - - - - - - -

Do you need a PASSPORT? Draw it here.
If you're not going abroad, you could design your own!

These days, everyone needs a **passport** to travel abroad. These little booklets are filled with information about our nationality, the date and place of our birth, and a close-up photograph of our face.

Although the passport as we know it was only invented in the early 20th century, its name is taken from the documents travelers needed to **"pass"** through **"ports"** or city gates as long as 500 years ago.

# YOU'VE ARRIVED!

Where are you staying?
(You can underline as many words as you need to!)

>> With relatives or friends.

>> At camp, on a school break.

>> In a hotel or vacation rental.

>> On a boat, in a tent, or in another unusual place.

Describe the place you're staying here:

- - - - - - - - - - - - - - - - - - - - - - - - - - - - - - - -

- - - - - - - - - - - - - - - - - - - - - - - - - - - - - - - -

When we travel, things often look strange and new.
Find something that looks different, and draw it here.
You could choose a road sign, a packet of food, a plant,
or anything else you find that seems interesting!

This is a picture of:

- - - - - - - - - - - - - - - - - - - - - - - - - - - - - -

The biggest hotel in the world is the **First World Hotel and Plaza** in **Malaysia**, which has a total of **7,351 rooms**.

# A DAY OUT

Use this book to record what you do for a day.

First, what's the DATE?

- - - - - - - - - - - - - - - - - - - - - - - - - - - - - - -

WHERE are you going today?

- - - - - - - - - - - - - - - - - - - - - - - - - - - - - - -

- - - - - - - - - - - - - - - - - - - - - - - - - - - - - - -

WHO are you going with?

- - - - - - - - - - - - - - - - - - - - - - - - - - - - - - -

- - - - - - - - - - - - - - - - - - - - - - - - - - - - - - -

>> Describe your day here.

Make a note of what you do at these different times:

9.00 am:

- - - - - - - - - - - - - - - - - - - - - - - - - - -

11.00 am:

- - - - - - - - - - - - - - - - - - - - - - - - - - -

Lunch (you could write down what you ATE):

- - - - - - - - - - - - - - - - - - - - - - - - - - -

- - - - - - - - - - - - - - - - - - - - - - - - - - -

3.00 pm:

- - - - - - - - - - - - - - - - - - - - - - - - - - -

7.00 pm:

- - - - - - - - - - - - - - - - - - - - - - - - - - -

9.00 pm:

- - - - - - - - - - - - - - - - - - - - - - - - - - -

>> What was the BEST thing about today?

- - - - - - - - - - - - - - - - - - - - - - - - - - -

# VACATION GALLERY

DRAW your favorite VACATION MOMENTS here!
Make a note of what they are underneath.

# A TRIP TO REMEMBER...

Your trip is nearly over. It's time to make some lists!

>> What were the four BEST things about your trip?

- - - - - - - - - - - - - - - - - - - - - - - - - - - - - - -

- - - - - - - - - - - - - - - - - - - - - - - - - - - - - - -

- - - - - - - - - - - - - - - - - - - - - - - - - - - - - - -

- - - - - - - - - - - - - - - - - - - - - - - - - - - - - - -

>> Now write down four things you're looking forward to doing when you get home:

- - - - - - - - - - - - - - - - - - - - - - - - - - - - - - -

- - - - - - - - - - - - - - - - - - - - - - - - - - - - - - -

- - - - - - - - - - - - - - - - - - - - - - - - - - - - - - -

- - - - - - - - - - - - - - - - - - - - - - - - - - - - - - -

>> Finally, design a POSTER for the place you've visited. Think about what would make other people want to go there.

Save this space to draw a special vacation moment! What is it?

- - - - - - - - - - - - - - - - - - - - - - - - - - - - - -

# ADVENTURE NO.2

VACATION DESTINATION:

- - - - - - - - - - - - - - - - - - - - - - - - - - - - - - -

DATES you'll be away:

- - - - - - - - - - - - - - - - - - - - - - - - - - - - - - -

WHO are you traveling with? Are you VISITING anyone?

- - - - - - - - - - - - - - - - - - - - - - - - - - - - - - -

- - - - - - - - - - - - - - - - - - - - - - - - - - - - - - -

What are you HOPING TO SEE?

- - - - - - - - - - - - - - - - - - - - - - - - - - - - - - -

- - - - - - - - - - - - - - - - - - - - - - - - - - - - - - -

How are you GETTING THERE?

- - - - - - - - - - - - - - - - - - - - - - - - - - - - - - -

# PLANNING YOUR TRIP

Find out a little about the place you're going to.

How many PEOPLE live there?

- - - - - - - - - - - - - - - - - - - - - - - - - - - - - -

What's the TIME DIFFERENCE from your home town?

- - - - - - - - - - - - - - - - - - - - - - - - - - - - - -

Which other COUNTRIES or TOWNS are nearby?

- - - - - - - - - - - - - - - - - - - - - - - - - - - - - -

What's the most popular ATTRACTION?

- - - - - - - - - - - - - - - - - - - - - - - - - - - - - -

Are any FAMOUS BOOKS set in this place?

- - - - - - - - - - - - - - - - - - - - - - - - - - - - - -

DRAW the FLAG of the country you're visiting HERE.
(It might be the flag of your own country!)
Can you find out any facts about the flag?

>> Flag facts:

- - - - - - - - - - - - - - - - - - - - - - - - - - - - - - - - - - - - - - - -

- - - - - - - - - - - - - - - - - - - - - - - - - - - - - - - - - - - - - - - -

Every country in the world has its own **flag**. In the past, flags were used to identify nations in battle. They were also tied to the masts of sailing ships so that other crews could spot them from a distance. Most modern flags are made from blocks of color, stripes, and symbols.

In the flag of ARGENTINA, the motif of the sun with a human face represents Inti, the Inca sun god.

# PACKING LIST

Let's work out what you'll need for your trip.
You can look back to your last packing list if you like!

How long will you be staying?

- - - - - - - - - - - - - - - - - - - - - - - - - - - - - -

What's the weather forecast?

- - - - - - - - - - - - - - - - - - - - - - - - - - - - - -

DRAW your favorite VACATION CLOTHES here!

CIRCLE all the things you'll need to take with you!

socks (how many?)_ _ _ _ _ _     tops (how many?) _ _ _ _ _ _

underwear (how many?)_ _ _     pants (how many?)  _ _ _ _

pajamas (how many?) _ _ _ _     skirts (how many?)_ _ _ _ _

| warm coat | raincoat | sweater |
|-----------|----------|---------|
| beanie | gloves | scarf |
| toothbrush | toothpaste | soap |
| bathing suit | goggles | bodyboard |
| sunglasses | sunscreen | sunhat |
| shoes | sandals | boots |

>> Make a note of anything else you'll need:

_ _ _ _ _ _ _ _ _ _ _ _ _ _ _ _ _ _ _ _ _ _ _ _ _ _ _ _ _ _ _ _ _ _

_ _ _ _ _ _ _ _ _ _ _ _ _ _ _ _ _ _ _ _ _ _ _ _ _ _ _ _ _ _ _ _ _ _

_ _ _ _ _ _ _ _ _ _ _ _ _ _ _ _ _ _ _ _ _ _ _ _ _ _ _ _ _ _ _ _ _ _

_ _ _ _ _ _ _ _ _ _ _ _ _ _ _ _ _ _ _ _ _ _ _ _ _ _ _ _ _ _ _ _ _ _

You'll also want to pack THIS BOOK!

# GETTING THERE

How are you getting to your DESTINATION?

Circle as many ways of traveling as you need to:

>> CAR          >> CAMPERVAN or R.V.

>> BUS          >> AIRPLANE

>> BOAT         >> TRAIN

What DISTANCE will you be traveling?

- - - - - - - - - - - - - - - miles

How LONG will your journey take?

- - - - - - - - - - - - - -

Will you be passing through any places on the way?
Make a list of them:

- - - - - - - - - - - - - - - - - - - - - - - - - - - - - - -

- - - - - - - - - - - - - - - - - - - - - - - - - - - - - - -

- - - - - - - - - - - - - - - - - - - - - - - - - - - - - - -

>> Draw a map of the journey you'll be taking here:

The first **travel agents** appeared in the 19th century. In England, a former preacher called Thomas Cook worked with railway companies to organize trips by train for workers in northern cities. He believed that their lives would be improved by travel to new places.

Cook transported more than 150,000 people to the Great Exhibition in London's Hyde Park in 1851. Over the next decade his company began running "package" holidays abroad. It's still operating today.

# YOU'VE ARRIVED!

Where are you staying?
You can underline as many words as you need to!

>> With relatives or friends.

>> In a hotel or vacation rental.

>> At camp, on a school break.

>> On a boat, in a tent, or in another unusual place.

Describe the place you're staying here:

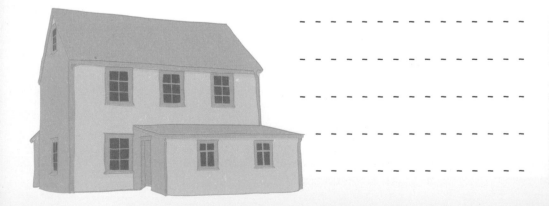

- - - - - - - - - - - - - - - -

- - - - - - - - - - - - - - - -

- - - - - - - - - - - - - - - -

- - - - - - - - - - - - - - - -

- - - - - - - - - - - - - - - -

Draw a picture of the ROOM you're staying in here.
Are you sharing with anyone? You can draw them in the
picture, too. Remember to include anything that looks
different to your room at home.

In **Costa Verde, Costa Rica**, travelers can stay in a converted Boeing 727 airplane, which is half buried in jungle, in the trees of the Manuel Antonio National Park.

# A DAY OUT

Use this book to record what you do for a day.

First, what's the DATE?

- - - - - - - - - - - - - - - - - - - - - - - - - - - - -

WHERE are you going today?

- - - - - - - - - - - - - - - - - - - - - - - - - - - - -

- - - - - - - - - - - - - - - - - - - - - - - - - - - - -

WHO are you going with?

- - - - - - - - - - - - - - - - - - - - - - - - - - - - -

- - - - - - - - - - - - - - - - - - - - - - - - - - - - -

It's not hard to find ice cream on vacation these days! But it used to be considered a rare treat. There are stories of **frozen desserts** being enjoyed as far back as the 16th century in the court of the Italian noblewoman Catherine de Medici, who became Queen of France in 1547.

>> What did you EAT today?
Did you eat any food you've never had before?

BREAKFAST at_ _ _ _ _ _am:

What I ate:

- - - - - - - - - - - - - - - - - - - - - - - - - - - -

- - - - - - - - - - - - - - - - - - - - - - - - - - - -

LUNCH at_ _ _ _ _ _am:

What I ate:

- - - - - - - - - - - - - - - - - - - - - - - - - - - -

- - - - - - - - - - - - - - - - - - - - - - - - - - - -

DINNER at_ _ _ _ _ _am:

What I ate:

- - - - - - - - - - - - - - - - - - - - - - - - - - - -

- - - - - - - - - - - - - - - - - - - - - - - - - - - -

>> What was the BEST thing about today?

- - - - - - - - - - - - - - - - - - - - - - - - - - - -

- - - - - - - - - - - - - - - - - - - - - - - - - - - -

- - - - - - - - - - - - - - - - - - - - - - - - - - - -

# VACATION GALLERY

DRAW some special VACATION MOMENTS here!

# A TRIP TO REMEMBER...

Your trip is nearly over. It's time to make some lists!

>> Make a note of four INTERESTING THINGS you spotted on your vacation:

- - - - - - - - - - - - - - - - - - - - - - - - - - - -

- - - - - - - - - - - - - - - - - - - - - - - - - - - -

- - - - - - - - - - - - - - - - - - - - - - - - - - - -

- - - - - - - - - - - - - - - - - - - - - - - - - - - -

>> And four DIFFERENCES between the place you've been on vacation and where you live at home:

- - - - - - - - - - - - - - - - - - - - - - - - - - - -

- - - - - - - - - - - - - - - - - - - - - - - - - - - -

- - - - - - - - - - - - - - - - - - - - - - - - - - - -

>> Finally, plan a POSTCARD to send to someone close to you. It could be the person you've missed the most!

Dear _ _ _ _ _ _ _ _ _ _ _ _ _ _ _ _ _ _ _ _ _

Today I went to _ _ _ _ _ _ _ _ _ _ _ _ _ _ _ _ _ _

and enjoyed looking at _ _ _ _ _ _ _ _ _ _ _ _ _ _ _

which made me think about _ _ _ _ _ _ _ _ _ _ _ _ _ _

Looking forward to telling you all about my trip!

From _ _ _ _ _ _ _ _ _ _ _ _ _ _ _ _ _ _

The coastline and islands of the **Mediterranean Sea** are among the world's most popular vacation destinations. In Latin the word means "in the middle of the earth." Traders and travelers from ancient civilizations sailed across this sea thousands of years ago. It is surrounded by many countries including Spain, Morocco, Egypt, Italy, Turkey, and Greece.

Save this space to draw a special vacation moment! What is it?

- - - - - - - - - - - - - - - - - - - - - - - - - - - - -

# ADVENTURE NO.3

VACATION DESTINATION:

- - - - - - - - - - - - - - - - - - - - - - - - - - - - - - - -

DATES you'll be away:

- - - - - - - - - - - - - - - - - - - - - - - - - - - - - - - -

WHO are you traveling with? Are you VISITING anyone?

- - - - - - - - - - - - - - - - - - - - - - - - - - - - - - - -

- - - - - - - - - - - - - - - - - - - - - - - - - - - - - - - -

What are you HOPING TO SEE?

- - - - - - - - - - - - - - - - - - - - - - - - - - - - - - - -

- - - - - - - - - - - - - - - - - - - - - - - - - - - - - - - -

How are you GETTING THERE?

- - - - - - - - - - - - - - - - - - - - - - - - - - - - - - - -

# PLANNING YOUR TRIP

Find out a little about the place you're going to.

Is it near any RIVERS or LAKES? What are they?

- - - - - - - - - - - - - - - - - - - - - - - - - -

Is it famous for any particular FOOD or DRINK?

- - - - - - - - - - - - - - - - - - - - - - - - - -

What's the WEATHER usually like?

- - - - - - - - - - - - - - - - - - - - - - - - - -

What ANIMALS live there?

- - - - - - - - - - - - - - - - - - - - - - - - - -

DRAW a famous landmark from the place you'll be visiting HERE. Can you find out an interesting fact about it?

This is a picture of:

- - - - - - - - - - - - - - - - - - - - - - - - - - - - - - - - - -

which is famous for:

- - - - - - - - - - - - - - - - - - - - - - - - - - - - - - - - - -

- - - - - - - - - - - - - - - - - - - - - - - - - - - - - - - - - -

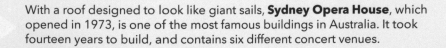

With a roof designed to look like giant sails, **Sydney Opera House**, which opened in 1973, is one of the most famous buildings in Australia. It took fourteen years to build, and contains six different concert venues.

# PACKING LIST

Let's work out what you'll need for your trip.
How long will you be staying?

- - - - - - - - - - - - - - - - - - - - - - - - - - - - - - - - -

DRAW what you'll take with you on the journey
here. (You might like something to read or some
music to listen to.)

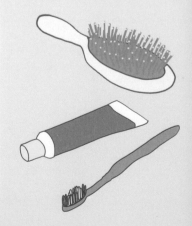

CIRCLE all the things you'll need to take with you!

socks (how many?) _ _ _ _ _ _          tops (how many?) _ _ _ _ _ _

underwear (how many?) _ _ _          pants (how many?) _ _ _ _

pajamas (how many?) _ _ _ _          skirts (how many?) _ _ _ _ _

| | | |
|---|---|---|
| warm coat | raincoat | sweater |
| beanie | gloves | scarf |
| toothbrush | toothpaste | soap |
| bathing suit | goggles | bodyboard |
| sunglasses | sunscreen | sunhat |
| shoes | sandals | boots |

>> Make a note of anything else you'll need:

_ _ _ _ _ _ _ _ _ _ _ _ _ _ _ _ _ _ _ _ _ _ _ _ _ _ _ _ _ _ _ _

_ _ _ _ _ _ _ _ _ _ _ _ _ _ _ _ _ _ _ _ _ _ _ _ _ _ _ _ _ _ _ _

_ _ _ _ _ _ _ _ _ _ _ _ _ _ _ _ _ _ _ _ _ _ _ _ _ _ _ _ _ _ _ _

_ _ _ _ _ _ _ _ _ _ _ _ _ _ _ _ _ _ _ _ _ _ _ _ _ _ _ _ _ _ _ _

You'll also want to pack THIS BOOK!

# GETTING THERE

How are you getting to your DESTINATION?

Circle as many ways of traveling as you need to:

>> CAR          >> CAMPERVAN or R.V.

>> BUS          >> AIRPLANE

>> BOAT         >> TRAIN

How FAR will you be traveling?

- - - - - - - - - - - miles

WHO will you be traveling with?

- - - - - - - - - - - - - - - - - - - - - - - - - - - - - - - -

- - - - - - - - - - - - - - - - - - - - - - - - - - - - - - - -

- - - - - - - - - - - - - - - - - - - - - - - - - - - - - - - -

Can you invent a TRAVEL GAME to play on the way?

Write the rules here:

- - - - - - - - - - - - - - - - - - - - - - - - - - - - - - - -

- - - - - - - - - - - - - - - - - - - - - - - - - - - - - - - -

- - - - - - - - - - - - - - - - - - - - - - - - - - - - - - - -

- - - - - - - - - - - - - - - - - - - - - - - - - - - - - - - -

- - - - - - - - - - - - - - - - - - - - - - - - - - - - - - - -

- - - - - - - - - - - - - - - - - - - - - - - - - - - - - - - -

How LONG will your journey take?

- - - - - - - - - - - - - - - - - - - -

# YOU'VE ARRIVED!

Where are you staying?
(You can underline as many words as you need to!)

>> With relatives or friends.

>> In a hotel or vacation rental.

>> At camp, on a school break.

>> On a boat, in a tent or in another unusual place.


Describe the place you're staying here:

- - - - - - - - - - - - - - - - - - - - - - - - - - - -

- - - - - - - - - - - - - - - - - - - - - - - - - - - -

- - - - - - - - - - - - - - - - - - - - - - - - - - - -

- - - - - - - - - - - - - - - - - - - - - - - - - - - -

Draw the view from your window here.

In the north of **Sweden** it's possible to stay in a hotel made of **ice**! Guests at the Ice Hotel, which has to be created every winter, are offered the choice of cold or warm rooms – and cozy clothes can be provided.

# A DAY OUT

Use this book to record what you do for a day.

First, what's the DATE?

- - - - - - - - - - - - - - - - - - - - - - - - - - - - - -

WHERE are you going today?

- - - - - - - - - - - - - - - - - - - - - - - - - - - - - -

- - - - - - - - - - - - - - - - - - - - - - - - - - - - - -

WHO are you going with?

- - - - - - - - - - - - - - - - - - - - - - - - - - - - - -

- - - - - - - - - - - - - - - - - - - - - - - - - - - - - -

WHAT is the weather like?

- - - - - - - - - - - - - - - - - - - - - - - - - - - - - -

- - - - - - - - - - - - - - - - - - - - - - - - - - - - - -

Make a note of any ACTIVITIES you do today:

- - - - - - - - - - - - - - - - - - - - - - - - - - - - - - - -

- - - - - - - - - - - - - - - - - - - - - - - - - - - - - - - -

>> You can DESIGN your own CLIMBING WALL below!

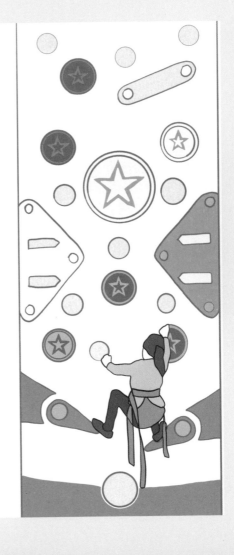

# VACATION
# GALLERY

DRAW your favorite VACATION MOMENTS here!
Make a note of what they are underneath.

# A TRIP TO REMEMBER...

Your trip is nearly over. It's time to make some lists!

>> What were the four FUNNIEST moments on your vacation:

- - - - - - - - - - - - - - - - - - - - - - - - - - - - - -

- - - - - - - - - - - - - - - - - - - - - - - - - - - - - -

- - - - - - - - - - - - - - - - - - - - - - - - - - - - - -

- - - - - - - - - - - - - - - - - - - - - - - - - - - - - -

>> What were your four BEST vacation activities?

- - - - - - - - - - - - - - - - - - - - - - - - - - - - - -

- - - - - - - - - - - - - - - - - - - - - - - - - - - - - -

- - - - - - - - - - - - - - - - - - - - - - - - - - - - - -

- - - - - - - - - - - - - - - - - - - - - - - - - - - - - -

>> Finally, draw something (or someone) that you
CAN'T WAIT TO SEE when you get back home!

Save this space to draw a special vacation moment! What is it?

- - - - - - - - - - - - - - - - - - - - - - - - - - - - - - -

# ADVENTURE NO.4

VACATION DESTINATION:

- - - - - - - - - - - - - - - - - - - - - - - - - - - - - - - - - - - - -

DATES you'll be away:

- - - - - - - - - - - - - - - - - - - - - - - - - - - - - - - - - - - - -

WHO are you traveling with? Are you VISITING
anyone?

- - - - - - - - - - - - - - - - - - - - - - - - - - - - - - - - - - - - -

- - - - - - - - - - - - - - - - - - - - - - - - - - - - - - - - - - - - -

What are you HOPING TO SEE?

- - - - - - - - - - - - - - - - - - - - - - - - - - - - - - - - - - - - -

- - - - - - - - - - - - - - - - - - - - - - - - - - - - - - - - - - - - -

How are you GETTING THERE?

- - - - - - - - - - - - - - - - - - - - - - - - - - - - - - - - - - - - -

# PLANNING YOUR TRIP

Find out a little about the place you're going to.

Is it in the COUNTRYSIDE or in a CITY?

- - - - - - - - - - - - - - - - - - - - - - - - - - - - - -

Do any special PLANTS or TREES grow there?

- - - - - - - - - - - - - - - - - - - - - - - - - - - - - -

Is it SUMMER or WINTER weather?

- - - - - - - - - - - - - - - - - - - - - - - - - - - - - -

Do cars drive on the LEFT or RIGHT side of the road?

- - - - - - - - - - - - - - - - - - - - - - - - - - - - - -

What will you see that you DON'T have at home?

- - - - - - - - - - - - - - - - - - - - - - - - - - - - - -

DRAW an ANIMAL that lives in the place you're visiting. What do they eat?

**Penguins** enjoy the cold climate of Antarctica, but they can also be found in parts of South America, South Africa, Australia, New Zealand, and even as far north as the Galapagos Islands.

These flightless birds were mentioned in the journals of the Portuguese voyager Alvaro Velho, who sailed around the Cape of Good Hope, at the southern tip of Africa, in 1497.

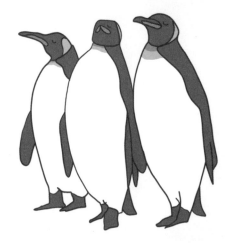

# PACKING LIST

Let's work out what you'll need for your trip.

How long will you be staying?

- - - - - - - - - - - - - - - - - - - - - - - - - - - - - - - -

What can't you leave behind? Draw it here!

CIRCLE all the things you'll need to take with you!

socks (how many?)_ _ _ _ _ _    tops (how many?) _ _ _ _ _ _

underwear (how many?) _ _ _    pants (how many?)    _ _ _ _

pajamas (how many?) _ _ _ _    skirts (how many?) _ _ _ _ _

| | | |
|---|---|---|
| warm coat | raincoat | sweater |
| beanie | gloves | scarf |
| toothbrush | toothpaste | soap |
| bathing suit | goggles | bodyboard |
| sunglasses | sunscreen | sunhat |
| shoes | sandals | boots |

>> Make a note of anything else you'll need:

- - - - - - - - - - - - - - - - - - - - - - - - - - - -

- - - - - - - - - - - - - - - - - - - - - - - - - - - -

- - - - - - - - - - - - - - - - - - - - - - - - - - - -

- - - - - - - - - - - - - - - - - - - - - - - - - - - -

Remember to pack THIS BOOK!

# GETTING THERE

How are you getting to your DESTINATION?

Circle as many ways of traveling as you need to:

>> CAR          >> CAMPERVAN or R.V.

>> BUS          >> AIRPLANE

>> BOAT         >> TRAIN

How many FAR will you be traveling?

- - - - - - - - - - - - - miles

How LONG will your journey take?

- - - - - - - - - - - - -

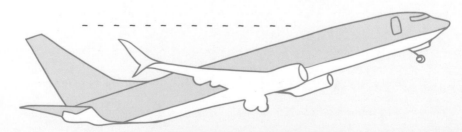

Start this page when you're ON YOUR JOURNEY.
Look at the seat you're sitting in and draw it here.

Now, draw the view from your WINDOW.

**Airports** are busy places! The **largest** airport in the USA is Denver International Airport. With six runways and an area of over 52 square miles, it's twice the size of Manhattan. Meanwhile, Hartsfield-Jackson Atlanta International Airport is the world's **busiest** airport. In 2019 over **110 million** people passed through it.

# YOU'VE ARRIVED!

Where are you staying?
(You can underline as many words as you need to!)

>> With relatives or friends.

>> In a hotel or vacation rental.

>> At camp, on a school break.

>> On a boat, in a tent or in another unusual place.

Describe the place you're staying here:

- - - - - - - - - - - - - - - - - - - - - - - - - -

- - - - - - - - - - - - - - - - - - - - - - - - - -

- - - - - - - - - - - - - - - - - - - - - - - - - -

- - - - - - - - - - - - - - - - - - - - - - - - - -

When we visit new places, we often notice new sounds and smells. Make a note of any interesting things here.

## VACATION SMELLS

- - - - - - - - - - - - - - - - - - - - - - - - - - - - -

- - - - - - - - - - - - - - - - - - - - - - - - - - - - -

- - - - - - - - - - - - - - - - - - - - - - - - - - - - -

- - - - - - - - - - - - - - - - - - - - - - - - - - - - -

## VACATION SOUNDS

- - - - - - - - - - - - - - - - - - - - - - - - - - - - -

- - - - - - - - - - - - - - - - - - - - - - - - - - - - -

- - - - - - - - - - - - - - - - - - - - - - - - - - - - -

- - - - - - - - - - - - - - - - - - - - - - - - - - - - -

Male **crickets** make their distinctive "chirping" song by scraping their wings together. The sound they make changes according to the temperature. As it gets hotter, their chirps speed up!

# A DAY OUT

Take this book out and record what you do for a day.
First, what's the DATE?

- - - - - - - - - - - - - - - - - - - - - - - - - - - - - -

WHAT are you visiting today?

- - - - - - - - - - - - - - - - - - - - - - - - - - - - - -

- - - - - - - - - - - - - - - - - - - - - - - - - - - - - -

WHO are you going with?

- - - - - - - - - - - - - - - - - - - - - - - - - - - - - -

- - - - - - - - - - - - - - - - - - - - - - - - - - - - - -

WHAT's the plan for today?

- - - - - - - - - - - - - - - - - - - - - - - - - - - - - -

- - - - - - - - - - - - - - - - - - - - - - - - - - - - - -

>> Describe your day here:

Make a note of what you did at these different times:

8.00 am:

- - - - - - - - - - - - - - - - - - - - - - - - - - - -

10.00 am:

- - - - - - - - - - - - - - - - - - - - - - - - - - - -

Lunch (you could make a note of what you ATE):

- - - - - - - - - - - - - - - - - - - - - - - - - - - -

2.00 pm:

- - - - - - - - - - - - - - - - - - - - - - - - - - - -

6.00 pm:

- - - - - - - - - - - - - - - - - - - - - - - - - - - -

8.00 pm:

- - - - - - - - - - - - - - - - - - - - - - - - - - - -


>> What was the BEST thing about today?

- - - - - - - - - - - - - - - - - - - - - - - - - - - -

# VACATION GALLERY

DRAW your favourite VACATION MOMENTS here!
Make a note of what they are underneath.

– – – – – – – – – – – – – – – – –

– – – – – – – – – – – – – – – – – – – – – – – – – – – –

# A TRIP TO REMEMBER...

Your trip is nearly over. It's time to make some lists!

>> What were the four BEST things about your trip?

- - - - - - - - - - - - - - - - - - - - - - - - - - - - - -

- - - - - - - - - - - - - - - - - - - - - - - - - - - - - -

- - - - - - - - - - - - - - - - - - - - - - - - - - - - - -

- - - - - - - - - - - - - - - - - - - - - - - - - - - - - -

>> Now write down four things you're looking forward to doing when you get HOME:

- - - - - - - - - - - - - - - - - - - - - - - - - - - - - -

- - - - - - - - - - - - - - - - - - - - - - - - - - - - - -

- - - - - - - - - - - - - - - - - - - - - - - - - - - - - -

- - - - - - - - - - - - - - - - - - - - - - - - - - - - - -

>> Before you leave, look around one last time. Write down all the words that spring to mind.

- - - - - - - - - - - - - - - - - - - - - - - - - - - - - - - - - - - - - - - -

- - - - - - - - - - - - - - - - - - - - - - - - - - - - - - - - - - - - - - - -

- - - - - - - - - - - - - - - - - - - - - - - - - - - - - - - - - - - - - - - -

- - - - - - - - - - - - - - - - - - - - - - - - - - - - - - - - - - - - - - - -

- - - - - - - - - - - - - - - - - - - - - - - - - - - - - - - - - - - - - - - -

- - - - - - - - - - - - - - - - - - - - - - - - - - - - - - - - - - - - - - - -

- - - - - - - - - - - - - - - - - - - - - - - - - - - - - - - - - - - - - - - -

- - - - - - - - - - - - - - - - - - - - - - - - - - - - - - - - - - - - - - - -

Save this space to draw a special vacation moment! What is it?

- - - - - - - - - - - - - - - - - - - - - - - - - - - - - -

# ADVENTURE NO.5

VACATION DESTINATION:

- - - - - - - - - - - - - - - - - - - - - - - - - - - - - - - - - - - -

DATES you'll be away:

- - - - - - - - - - - - - - - - - - - - - - - - - - - - - - - - - - - -

WHO are you traveling with? Are you VISITING
anyone?

- - - - - - - - - - - - - - - - - - - - - - - - - - - - - - - - - - - -

- - - - - - - - - - - - - - - - - - - - - - - - - - - - - - - - - - - -

What are you HOPING TO SEE?

- - - - - - - - - - - - - - - - - - - - - - - - - - - - - - - - - - - -

- - - - - - - - - - - - - - - - - - - - - - - - - - - - - - - - - - - -

How are you GETTING THERE?

- - - - - - - - - - - - - - - - - - - - - - - - - - - - - - - - - - - -

# PLANNING YOUR TRIP

Find out a little about the place you're going to.

How many PEOPLE live there?

- - - - - - - - - - - - - - - - - - - - - - - - - - - -

Is it famous for any particular FOOD or DRINK?

- - - - - - - - - - - - - - - - - - - - - - - - - - - -

Does it have any interesting CUSTOMS or FESTIVALS?

- - - - - - - - - - - - - - - - - - - - - - - - - - - -

Can you find out the name of a popular ATTRACTION?

- - - - - - - - - - - - - - - - - - - - - - - - - - - -

What's its most FAMOUS BUILDING?

- - - - - - - - - - - - - - - - - - - - - - - - - - - -

What was the place you're visiting like ONE HUNDRED YEARS AGO? Would you have been able to travel there then? Describe some of the differences here.

- - - - - - - - - - - - - - - - - - - - - - - - - - - - - - - - - - - - -

- - - - - - - - - - - - - - - - - - - - - - - - - - - - - - - - - - - - -

- - - - - - - - - - - - - - - - - - - - - - - - - - - - - - - - - - - - -

- - - - - - - - - - - - - - - - - - - - - - - - - - - - - - - - - - - - -

- - - - - - - - - - - - - - - - - - - - - - - - - - - - - - - - - - - - -

- - - - - - - - - - - - - - - - - - - - - - - - - - - - - - - - - - - - -

- - - - - - - - - - - - - - - - - - - - - - - - - - - - - - - - - - - - -

Colorful flowers like the **hibiscus** are often found on postcards! They grow in sunny, tropical climates and can be found in many countries around the world. The red hibiscus is the national flower of Malaysia, while its yellow cousin is the state flower of Hawaii.

Since ancient times hibiscus petals have been used in medicine - both Egyptian Pharaohs and Chinese Emperors drank hibiscus tea for its healing properties.

# PACKING LIST

Let's work out what you'll need for your trip.

How long will you be staying?

- - - - - - - - - - - - - - - - - - - - - - - - - - - - -

DRAW the cover of a BOOK you're planning to read on your vacation HERE. What's it called?

TITLE:

- - - - - - - - - - - - - -

BY:

- - - - - - - - - - - - - -

CIRCLE all the things you'll need to take with you!

socks (how many?)_ _ _ _ _ _      tops (how many?) _ _ _ _ _ _

underwear (how many?) _ _ _      pants (how many?)  _ _ _ _

pajamas (how many?) _ _ _ _      skirts (how many?)_ _ _ _ _

warm coat            raincoat            sweater

beanie               gloves              scarf

toothbrush           toothpaste          soap

bathing suit         goggles             bodyboard

sunglasses           sunscreen           sunhat

shoes                sandals             boots

>> Make a note of anything else you'll need:

- - - - - - - - - - - - - - - - - - - - - - - - - - - - - - -

- - - - - - - - - - - - - - - - - - - - - - - - - - - - - - -

- - - - - - - - - - - - - - - - - - - - - - - - - - - - - - -

- - - - - - - - - - - - - - - - - - - - - - - - - - - - - - -

You'll also want to pack THIS BOOK!

# GETTING THERE

How are you getting to your DESTINATION?

Circle as many ways of traveling as you need to:

>> CAR        >> CAMPERVAN or R.V.

>> BUS        >> AIRPLANE

>> BOAT       >> TRAIN

How LONG will your journey take?

- - - - - - - - - - - - - - - - - - - - - - - - - - - - -

Do you have to STOP anywhere on the way?

- - - - - - - - - - - - - - - - - - - - - - - - - - - - -

What time will you ARRIVE?

- - - - - - - - - - - - - - - - - - - - - - - - - - - - -

Ask the people traveling with you to tell you what they're most looking forward to doing on vacation.

Name:

‎- - - - - - - - - - - - - - - - - - - - - - - - - - - - -

Looking forward to:

‎- - - - - - - - - - - - - - - - - - - - - - - - - - - - -

Name:

‎- - - - - - - - - - - - - - - - - - - - - - - - - - - - -

Looking forward to:

‎- - - - - - - - - - - - - - - - - - - - - - - - - - - - -

Name:

‎- - - - - - - - - - - - - - - - - - - - - - - - - - - - -

Looking forward to:

‎- - - - - - - - - - - - - - - - - - - - - - - - - - - - -

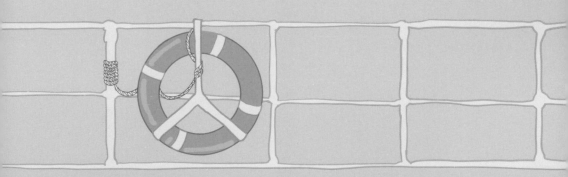

 Symphony of the Seas is the largest **cruise ship** in the world. It is 1,188 feet long, has 18 decks and has room for 6,680 passengers. There's space for a crew of over 2,000, too!

# YOU'VE ARRIVED!

Where are you staying?
(You can underline as many words as you need to!)

>> With relatives or friends.

>> In a hotel or vacation rental.

>> At camp, on a school break.

>> On a boat, in a tent, or in another unusual place.

Describe the place you're staying here:

- - - - - - - - - - - - - - - - - - - - - - - - - - - - -

- - - - - - - - - - - - - - - - - - - - - - - - - - - - -

Look around you. If you didn't know where you were, would you be able to guess? Draw all the things that might give you a clue HERE.

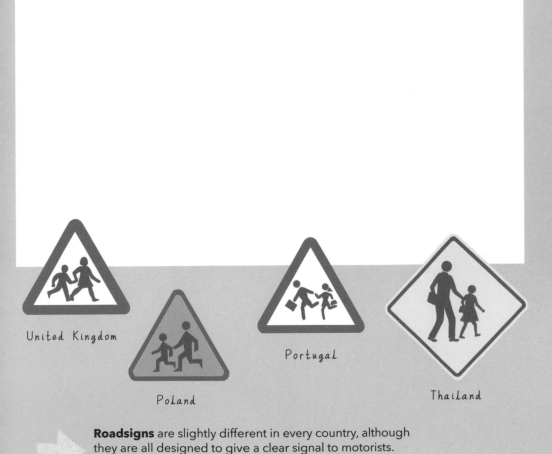

United Kingdom

Poland

Portugal

Thailand

**Roadsigns** are slightly different in every country, although they are all designed to give a clear signal to motorists. These signs all mean **caution, children present**.

# A DAY OUT

Use this book to record what you do for a day.

First, what's the DATE?

- - - - - - - - - - - - - - - - - - - - - - - - - - - -

WHERE are you going today?

- - - - - - - - - - - - - - - - - - - - - - - - - - - -

- - - - - - - - - - - - - - - - - - - - - - - - - - - -

WHO are you going with?

- - - - - - - - - - - - - - - - - - - - - - - - - - - -

>> Describe your day here.

Make a note of what you did at these different times:

9.00 am:

- - - - - - - - - - - - - - - - - - - - - - - - - - - - - -

11.00 am:

- - - - - - - - - - - - - - - - - - - - - - - - - - - - - -

Lunch (you could make a note of what you ATE):

- - - - - - - - - - - - - - - - - - - - - - - - - - - - - -

3.00 pm:

- - - - - - - - - - - - - - - - - - - - - - - - - - - - - -

7.00 pm:

- - - - - - - - - - - - - - - - - - - - - - - - - - - - - -

9.00 pm:

- - - - - - - - - - - - - - - - - - - - - - - - - - - - - -

>> What did you enjoy most today?

- - - - - - - - - - - - - - - - - - - - - - - - - - - - - -

# VACATION GALLERY

DRAW your favorite VACATION MOMENTS here!
Make a note of what they are underneath.

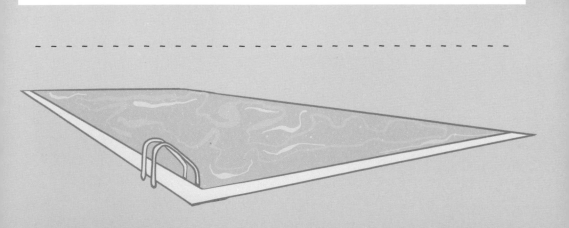

# A TRIP TO REMEMBER...

Your trip is nearly over. It's time to make some lists!

>> What were the four BEST places you visited?

- - - - - - - - - - - - - - - - - - - - - - - - - - - - - -

- - - - - - - - - - - - - - - - - - - - - - - - - - - - - -

- - - - - - - - - - - - - - - - - - - - - - - - - - - - - -

- - - - - - - - - - - - - - - - - - - - - - - - - - - - - -

>> Write down the names of any PEOPLE you MET.

- - - - - - - - - - - - - - - - - - - - - - - - - - - - - -

- - - - - - - - - - - - - - - - - - - - - - - - - - - - - -

- - - - - - - - - - - - - - - - - - - - - - - - - -

- - - - - - - - - - - - - - - - - - - - - - - - - -

>> Finally, can you plan a STORY about the place you've visited? Write down some ideas here. There's space for you to write out the whole story on the next page.

>> WHERE the action takes place:

- - - - - - - - - - - - - - - - - - - - - - - - - - - - - - -

- - - - - - - - - - - - - - - - - - - - - - - - - - - - - - -

>> NAMES of characters:

- - - - - - - - - - - - - - - - - - - - - - - - - - - - - - -

- - - - - - - - - - - - - - - - - - - - - - - - - - - - - - -

>> What happens at the BEGINNING?

- - - - - - - - - - - - - - - - - - - - - - - - - - - - - - -

- - - - - - - - - - - - - - - - - - - - - - - - - - - - - - -

>> And in the MIDDLE?

- - - - - - - - - - - - - - - - - - - - - - - - - - - - - - -

- - - - - - - - - - - - - - - - - - - - - - - - - - - - - - -

>> And at the END?

- - - - - - - - - - - - - - - - - - - - - - - - - - - - - - -

- - - - - - - - - - - - - - - - - - - - - - - - - - - - - - -

# MY VACATION STORY

- - - - - - - - - - - - - - - - - - - - - - - - - - - - - - - - -

- - - - - - - - - - - - - - - - - - - - - - - - - - - - - - - - -

- - - - - - - - - - - - - - - - - - - - - - - - - - - - - - - - -

- - - - - - - - - - - - - - - - - - - - - - - - - - - - - - - - -

- - - - - - - - - - - - - - - - - - - - - - - - - - - - - - - - -

- - - - - - - - - - - - - - - - - - - - - - - - - - - - - - - - -

- - - - - - - - - - - - - - - - - - - - - - - - - - - - - - - - -

- - - - - - - - - - - - - - - - - - - - - - - - - - - - - - - - -

- - - - - - - - - - - - - - - - - - - - - - - - - - - - - - - - -

- - - - - - - - - - - - - - - - - - - - - - - - - - - - - - - - -

- - - - - - - - - - - - - - - - - - - - - - - - - - - - - - - - -

- - - - - - - - - - - - - - - - - - - - - - - - - - - - - - - - -

- - - - - - - - - - - - - - - - - - - - - - - - - - - - - - - - -

- - - - - - - - - - - - - - - - - - - - - - - - - - - - - - - - -

- - - - - - - - - - - - - - - - - - - - - - - - - - - - - - - - -

- - - - - - - - - - - - - - - - - - - - - - - - - - - - - - - - - - - - - - - - - -

- - - - - - - - - - - - - - - - - - - - - - - - - - - - - - - - - - - - - - - - - -

- - - - - - - - - - - - - - - - - - - - - - - - - - - - - - - - - - - - - - - - - -

- - - - - - - - - - - - - - - - - - - - - - - - - - - - - - - - - - - - - - - - - -

- - - - - - - - - - - - - - - - - - - - - - - - - - - - - - - - - - - - - - - - - -

- - - - - - - - - - - - - - - - - - - - - - - - - - - - - - - - - - - - - - - - - -

- - - - - - - - - - - - - - - - - - - - - - - - - - - - - - - - - - - - - - - - - -

- - - - - - - - - - - - - - - - - - - - - - - - - - - - - - - - - - - - - - - - - -

You can DRAW a scene from your story here, too.

# YOUR VACATION ADVENTURES

You've finished your FIVE adventures!

>> Which was the BEST trip?

- - - - - - - - - - - - - - - - - - - - - - - - - - - - - -

>> Which place SURPRISED you the most?

- - - - - - - - - - - - - - - - - - - - - - - - - - - - - -

>> What was your favorite vacation ACTIVITY?

- - - - - - - - - - - - - - - - - - - - - - - - - - - - - -

>> Which place would you most like to visit again?

- - - - - - - - - - - - - - - - - - - - - - - - - - - - - -

>> Write down the name of TWO places you'd like to visit next. (You might need another copy of this book!)

- - - - - - - - - - - - - - - - - - - - - - - - - - - - - -

- - - - - - - - - - - - - - - - - - - - - - - - - - - - - -

Design your dream PLACE TO STAY here!

>> Where is it?

- - - - - - - - - - - - - - - - - - - - - - - - - - - - - - - -

>> And FINALLY, what's it called?

- - - - - - - - - - - - - - - - - - - - - - - - - - - - - - - -

This CERTIFICATE shows that

(name) - - - - - - - - - - - - - - - - - - - -

has visited FIVE incredible PLACES:

(1) - - - - - - - - - - - - - - - - - - - - -

(2) - - - - - - - - - - - - - - - - - - - - -

(3) - - - - - - - - - - - - - - - - - - - - -

(4) - - - - - - - - - - - - - - - - - - - - -

(5) - - - - - - - - - - - - - - - - - - - - -

signed

- - - - - - - - - - - - - - - - - - - - - - -

date

- - - - - - - - - - - - - - - - - - - - - - -